CHARACTER MENTOR STUDIO

Workbook 1:
Shape Inspiration

Tom Bancroft

For more information
on Character Design, other Workbooks in this series,
or to contact Tom Bancroft, please go to:
www.charactermentorstudio.com

Workbook 1 Instructions:

I created this workbook series with the thought that no matter your level of art ability or experiece, you never lack the need for inspiration. Workbook 1 is all about sparking your creativity.

Use the shapes provided in this workbook as a "design challenge" or inspiration to help "see" a new character! From there, its up to you. You can make any one of these shapes into the next big TV, comic strip, or film character! Each shape can be made into millions of differnt characters, so the sky is the limit. Buy multiple Workbook 1 workbooks and redo each assignment every month or two, you will see your growth as a character designer.

There are no rules to how you accomplish these shape challenges. You may want to take a legalistic approach and not go outside of the shape, or you may decide that adding a hat, neck, shoulders, or whatever on top of the shape is needed. It's up to you. Below is a few different ways I chose to approach the same shape as an example. Now, fill this workbook up with YOUR characters!

-Tom Bancroft,
Character Designer/ Animator/ Author-
"CREATING CHARACTERS WITH PERSONALITY"
and "CHARACTER MENTOR"

Shape
Example

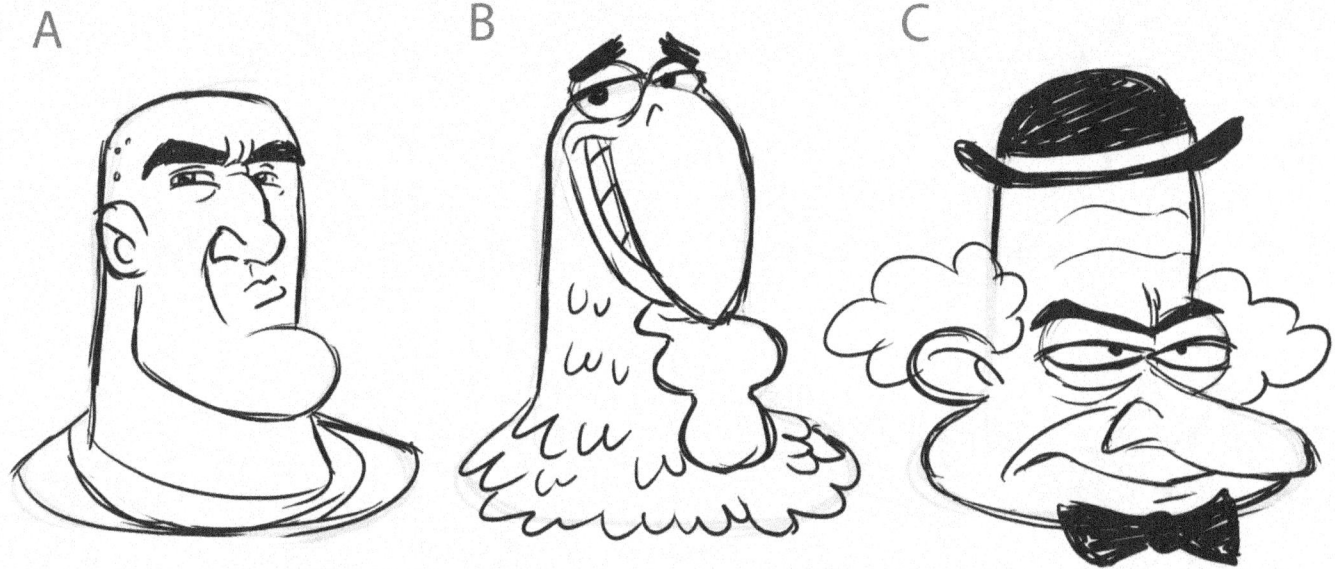

A   B   C

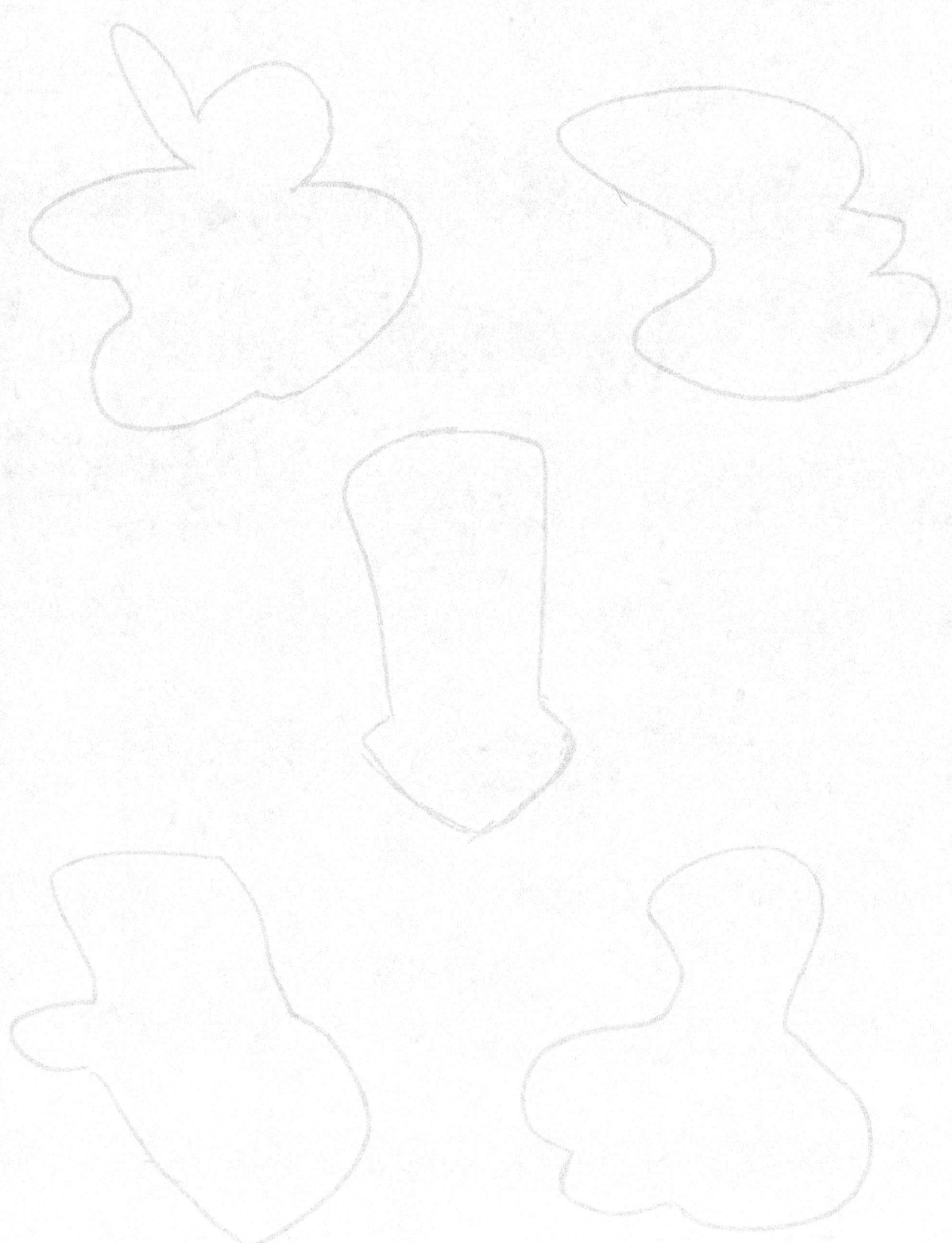

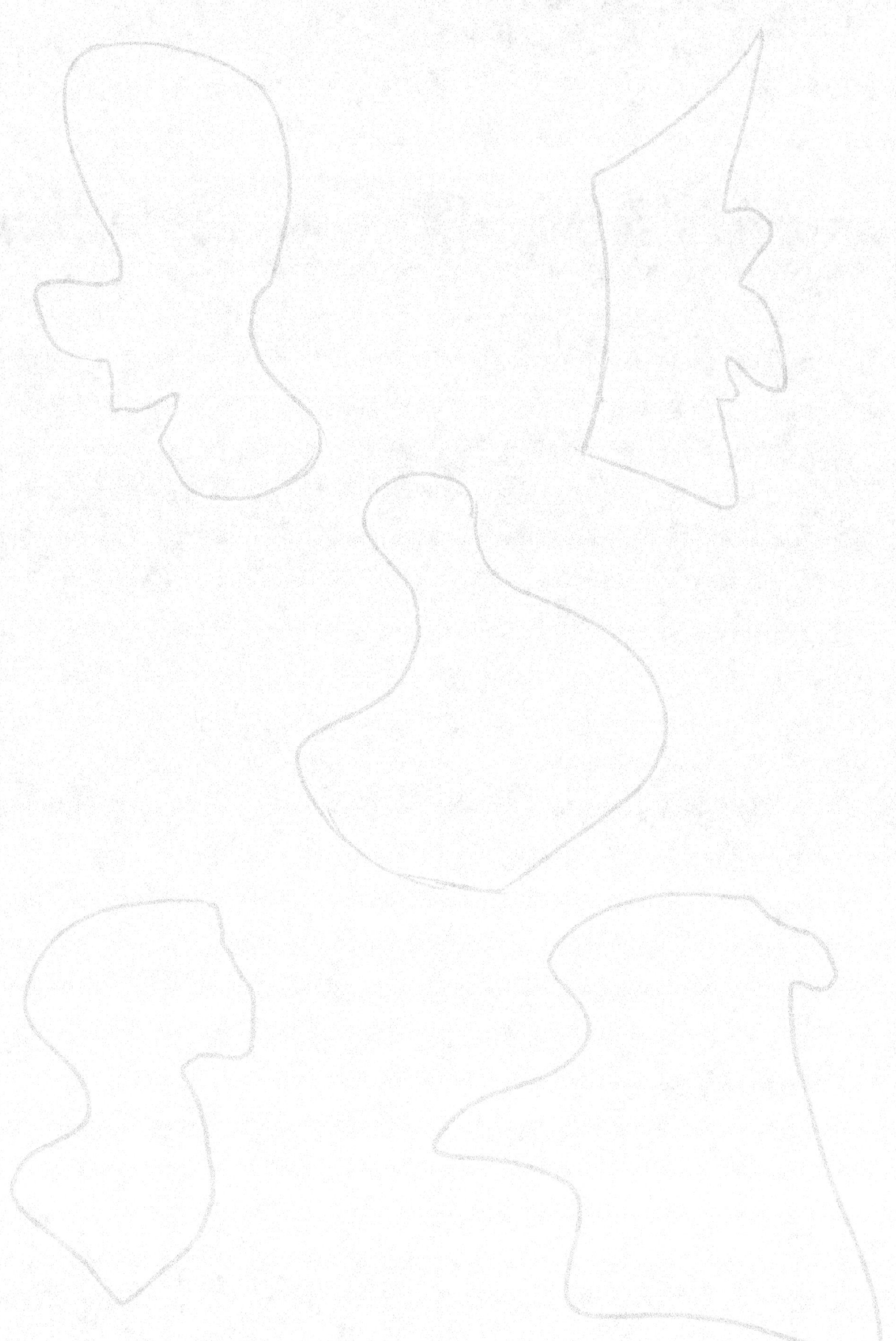

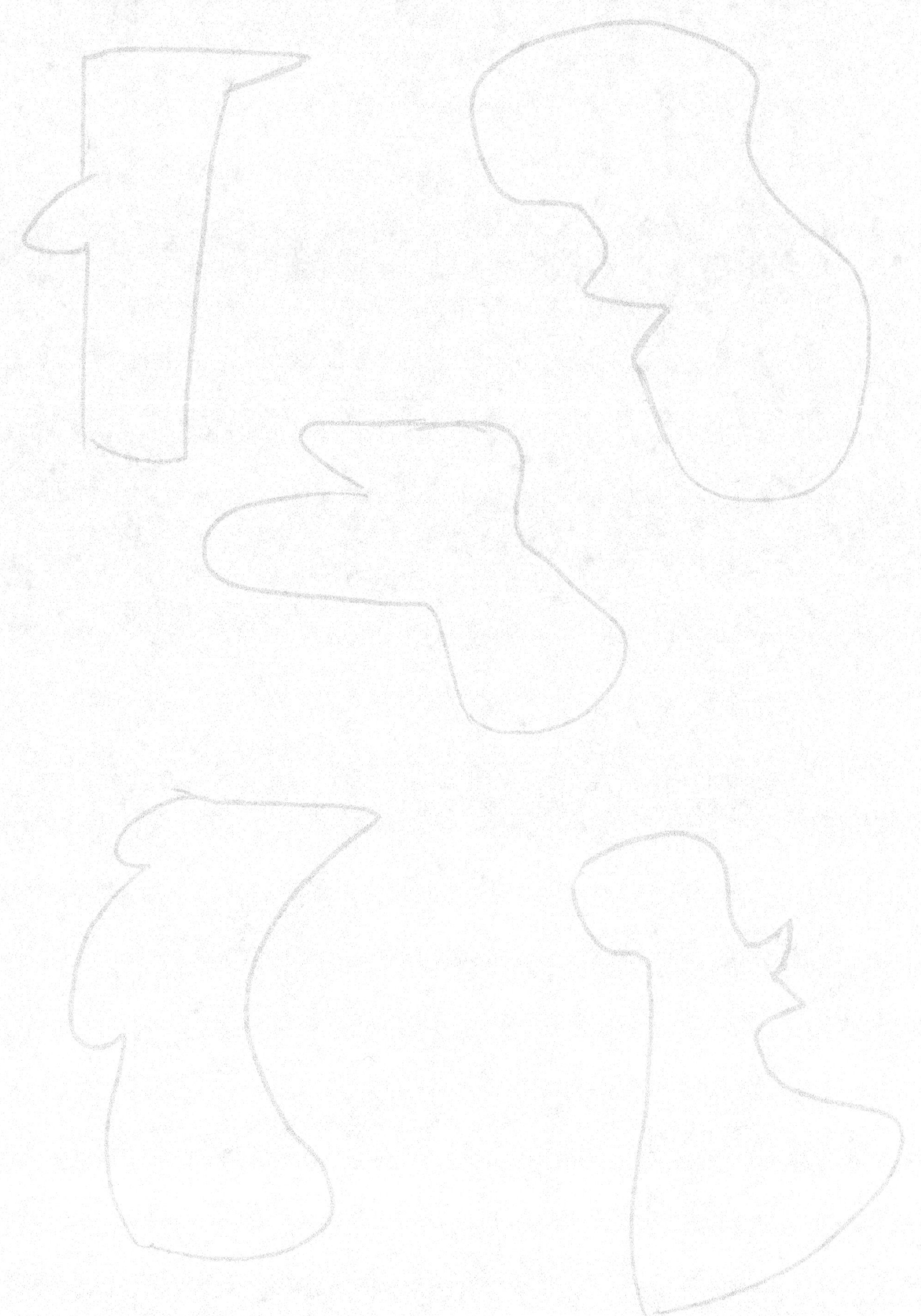

www.ingramcontent.com/pod-product-compliance
Lightning Source LLC
Chambersburg PA
CBHW081509170526
45166CB00008B/2598